My Family Estate Plan Record Book

Published By Martine J. Miller

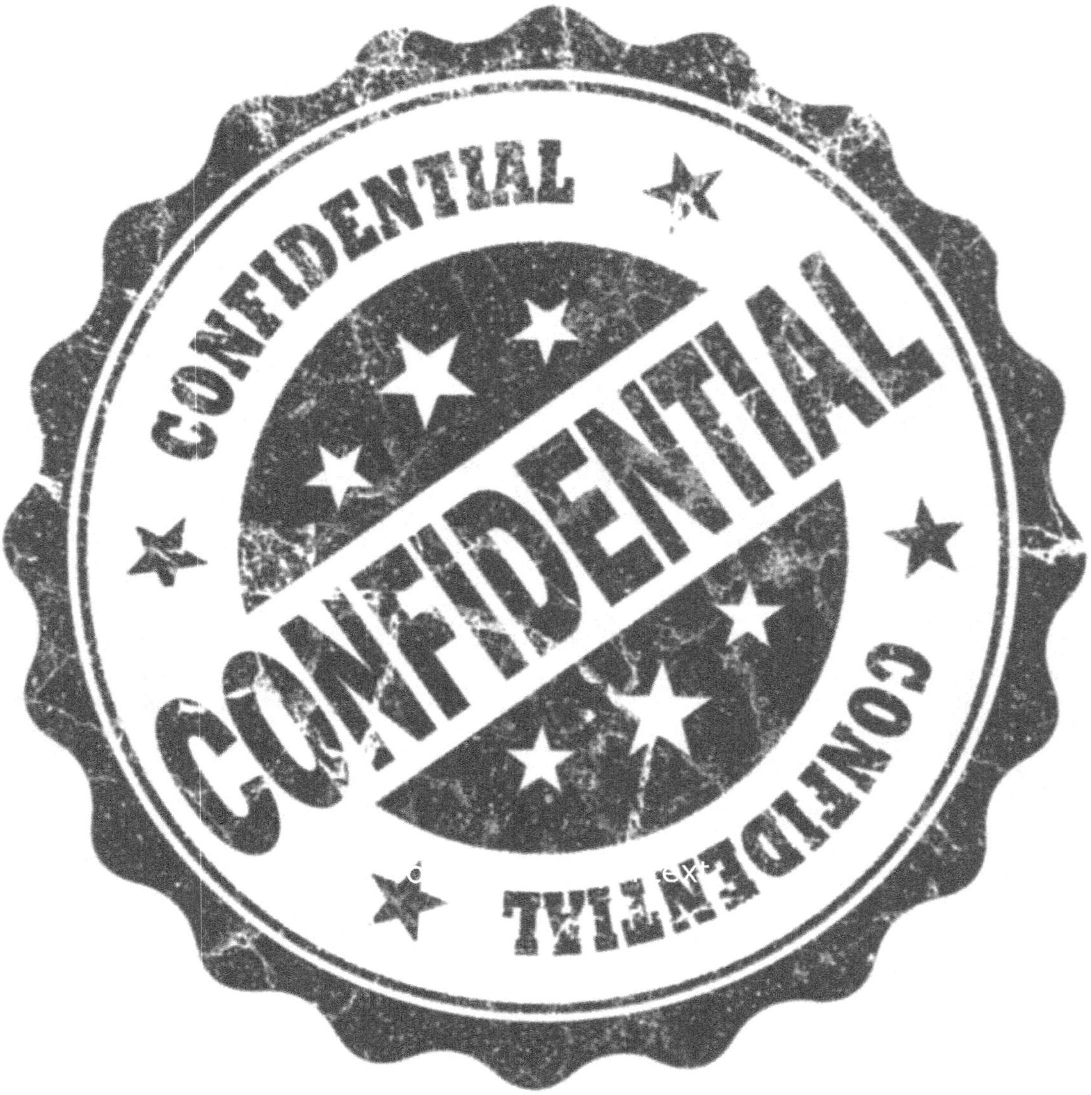

DISCLAIMER: It is always a good idea to consult with an attorney and/or your accountant to ensure that all your personal affairs have been handled in accordance with your final wishes and instructions.
If you have not yet made your Trust, Will and Last Testament, you should consult an attorney to get your affairs in order.

NOTE: This planner is not a legal document and does not replace a Final Will or Trust.

My Family Estate Plan Record Book

Belongs to

____

of

The ______________________________ Family

Date: ____/____/____

Purpose & How to Use This Record Book

This Record Book serves as a simple yet comprehensive tool to help your loved ones navigate important matters during times of transition. It goes beyond a will — ensuring that your wishes, assets, and instructions are clearly documented and easily accessible.

Maintaining this Estate Planning Record Book is a gift to those you love — offering clarity, reducing confusion, and easing the burdens that often arise during life's most challenging moments.

TABLE OF CONTENTS

DESCRIPTION | PAGES

Welcome & Quick Start Guide for

Your Family Estate Planning Record Book

Thanks for choosing this Estate Planning Record Book!
Getting organized now will make things much easier for you and your loved ones later.

Before You Begin

Take a few minutes to flip through the book. Some pages may not apply to you—and that's totally okay.

Protecting Your Book

For extra peace of mind, store your book in a safe place—like a waterproof, fireproof box.

Where to Keep It

Pick a secure, easy-to-find spot. Be sure to let a trusted family member, friend, or caregiver know where it is.

Keep It Updated

Life changes—your book should too. Check in regularly to update contacts, info, or documents as needed.

What This Book Is For

This isn't just about having a will—it's a guide to help your loved ones manage things smoothly if something unexpected happens. It's clear, simple, and made to support you and your family.

What is Included:

- Beneficiaries – Who gets what
- Assets – What you own (money, property, digital items)
- Guardianship – For kids or pets
- Power of Attorney – Who can make decisions for you
- Medical Directives – Your healthcare wishes
- Wills & Trusts – How to handle your estate
- Bills & Subscriptions – What to manage or cancel
- Passwords – Key logins to online accounts
- Funeral Wishes – Any special requests
- Important Documents – Where to find the big stuff (birth certificates, deeds, etc.)

Use this planner to help you stay on track!

Annual Review Log

DATE	UPDATED PAGE

DATE	UPDATED PAGE

DATE	UPDATED PAGE

DATE	UPDATED PAGE

DATE	UPDATED PAGE

FINAL WISHES

Final Wishes

To do

- ○
- ○
- ○
- ○
- ○
- ○
- ○
- ○

IN THIS AREA, YOU CAN PUT INFORMATION SUCH AS;
What kind of service would you like? (Funeral, memorial, celebration of life, or something simple)
Any special songs, readings, or prayers you'd like included? Where would you like the service to take place?
Who would you like to speak or be involved? Any Final Messages for Loved Ones? Should it be formal, casual, religious, or spiritual?
Do you prefer to be buried or cremated? If buried, do you already have a plot or location in mind?
If cremated, would you like your ashes scattered somewhere special or kept in an urn?

This is a chance to say what's in your heart.

Final Wishes

To do

- ○
- ○
- ○
- ○
- ○
- ○
- ○
- ○

IN THIS AREA, YOU CAN PUT INFORMATION SUCH AS;
What kind of service would you like? (Funeral, memorial, celebration of life, or something simple)
Any special songs, readings, or prayers you'd like included? Where would you like the service to take place?
Who would you like to speak or be involved? Any Final Messages for Loved Ones? Should it be formal, casual, religious, or spiritual?
Do you prefer to be buried or cremated? If buried, do you already have a plot or location in mind?
If cremated, would you like your ashes scattered somewhere special or kept in an urn?

This is a chance to say what's in your heart.

WILLS AND TRUSTS

CONTACT LIST

ATTORNEY CONTACT

Name: ______________________________

Phone: (________)____________________

Address: ____________________________

Email: ______________________________

FINANCIAL PLANNER CONTACT

Name: ______________________________

Phone: (________)____________________

Address: ____________________________

Email: ______________________________

ACCOUNTANT'S CONTACT

Name: ______________________________

Phone: (________)____________________

Address: ____________________________

Email: ______________________________

ADVANCED DIRECTIVES

○ ____________________ ○ ____________________

○ ____________________ ○ ____________________

○ ____________________ ○ ____________________

INFORMATION

DOCTOR

Name: ______________________________

Phone: (________)______________________

Address: ____________________________

Email: ______________________________

DOCTOR

Name: ______________________________

Phone: (________)______________________

Address: ____________________________

Email: ______________________________

DOCTOR

Name: ______________________________

Phone: (________)______________________

Address: ____________________________

Email: ______________________________

ANYTHING ELSE

○ ______________________ ○ ______________________

○ ______________________ ○ ______________________

○ ______________________ ○ ______________________

CONTACT LIST

Immediate Family

CONTACT LIST

Name: ______________________ Phone: (______)______________
Email: ______________________
Relationship: ______________ Date of Birth: ____/____/____ __ M __ F
Address: ____
Driver's License #: ______________________ State: __________

Name: ______________________ Phone: (______)______________
Email: ______________________
Relationship: ______________ Date of Birth: ____/____/____ __ M __ F
Address: ____
Driver's License #: ______________________ State: __________

Name: ______________________ Phone: (______)______________
Email: ______________________
Relationship: ______________ Date of Birth: ____/____/____ __ M __ F
Address: ____
Driver's License #: ______________________ State: __________

Name: ______________________ Phone: (______)______________
Email: ______________________
Relationship: ______________ Date of Birth: ____/____/____ __ M __ F
Address: ____
Driver's License #: ______________________ State: __________

Name: ______________________ Phone: (______)______________
Email: ______________________
Relationship: ______________ Date of Birth: ____/____/____ __ M __ F
Address: ____
Driver's License #: ______________________ State: __________

Immediate Family

CONTACT LIST

Name: ______________________ Phone: (______)______________
Email: ______________________
Relationship: ______________ Date of Birth: ____/____/____ __ M __ F
Address: ____
Driver's License #: ______________________ State: __________

Name: ______________________ Phone: (______)______________
Email: ______________________
Relationship: ______________ Date of Birth: ____/____/____ __ M __ F
Address: ____
Driver's License #: ______________________ State: __________

Name: ______________________ Phone: (______)______________
Email: ______________________
Relationship: ______________ Date of Birth: ____/____/____ __ M __ F
Address: ____
Driver's License #: ______________________ State: __________

Name: ______________________ Phone: (______)______________
Email: ______________________
Relationship: ______________ Date of Birth: ____/____/____ __ M __ F
Address: ____
Driver's License #: ______________________ State: __________

Name: ______________________ Phone: (______)______________
Email: ______________________
Relationship: ______________ Date of Birth: ____/____/____ __ M __ F
Address: ____
Driver's License #: ______________________ State: __________

Friends and Family
CONTACT LIST

Name: ______________________________

Phone: (________)__________________

Address: ______________________________
____

Email address: ______________________________

NOTES: ______________________________
____

Name: ______________________________

Phone: (________)__________________

Address: ______________________________
____

Email address: ______________________________

NOTES: ______________________________
____

Name: ______________________________

Phone: (________)__________________

Address: ______________________________
____

Email address: ______________________________

NOTES: ______________________________
____

Name: ______________________________

Phone: (________)__________________

Address: ______________________________
____

Email address: ______________________________

NOTES: ______________________________
____

Name: ______________________________

Phone: (________)__________________

Address: ______________________________
____

Email address: ______________________________

NOTES: ______________________________
____

Name: ______________________________

Phone: (________)__________________

Address: ______________________________
____

Email address: ______________________________

NOTES: ______________________________
____

Friends and Family

CONTACT LIST

Name: ______________________________

Phone: (________)____________________

Address: ____________________________

____

Email address: ______________________

NOTES: _____________________________

____

Name: ______________________________

Phone: (________)____________________

Address: ____________________________

____

Email address: ______________________

NOTES: _____________________________

____

Name: ______________________________

Phone: (________)____________________

Address: ____________________________

____

Email address: ______________________

NOTES: _____________________________

____

Name: ______________________________

Phone: (________)____________________

Address: ____________________________

____

Email address: ______________________

NOTES: _____________________________

____

Name: ______________________________

Phone: (________)____________________

Address: ____________________________

____

Email address: ______________________

NOTES: _____________________________

____

Name: ______________________________

Phone: (________)____________________

Address: ____________________________

____

Email address: ______________________

NOTES: _____________________________

____

ACCOUNTS

Bank Accounts

INFORMATION

Name of Bank: ______
Phone: (______)______
Address: ______
______
Routing #: ______ Account #: ______
Type of Account: Business ____ Personal ____
Checking ____ Savings ____ Other: ______
Name on Account: ______
Phone: (______)______
Email: ______
Website: ______
Login information: UserName: ______
Password: ______

Name of Bank: ______
Phone: (______)______
Address: ______
______
Routing #: ______ Account #: ______
Type of Account: Business ____ Personal ____
Checking ____ Savings ____ Other: ______
Name on Account: ______
Phone: (______)______
Email: ______
Website: ______
Login information: UserName: ______
Password: ______

Name of Bank: ______
Phone: (______)______
Address: ______
______
Routing #: ______ Account #: ______
Type of Account: Business ____ Personal ____
Checking ____ Savings ____ Other: ______
Name on Account: ______
Phone: (______)______
Email: ______
Website: ______
Login information: UserName: ______
Password: ______

Name of Bank: ______
Phone: (______)______
Address: ______
______
Routing #: ______ Account #: ______
Type of Account: Business ____ Personal ____
Checking ____ Savings ____ Other: ______
Name on Account: ______
Phone: (______)______
Email: ______
Website: ______
Login information: UserName: ______
Password: ______

Name of Bank: ______
Phone: (______)______
Address: ______
______
Routing #: ______ Account #: ______
Type of Account: Business ____ Personal ____
Checking ____ Savings ____ Other: ______
Name on Account: ______
Phone: (______)______
Email: ______
Website: ______
Login information: UserName: ______
Password: ______

Name of Bank: ______
Phone: (______)______
Address: ______
______
Routing #: ______ Account #: ______
Type of Account: Business ____ Personal ____
Checking ____ Savings ____ Other: ______
Name on Account: ______
Phone: (______)______
Email: ______
Website: ______
Login information: UserName: ______
Password: ______

Safety Deposit Box

CDS, SAVINGS, BONDS & MUTUAL FUNDS

SAFETY DEPOSIT BOX

Name of Bank: ______
Phone: (____)______
Address: ______
______
Account Name: ______
Phone: (____)______
Box #: ______
Where is the Key: ______
What's in the box: ______
______

Name of Bank: ______
Phone: (____)______
Address: ______
______
Account Name: ______
Phone: (____)______
Box #: ______
Where is the Key: ______
What's in the box: ______
______

CDs, SAVINGS BONDS AND MUTUAL FUNDS

Name of Bank: ______
Phone: (____)______
Address: ______
______
Type of Bond/Account: ______
Value: $______ Serial #: ______
Issue Date: ___/___/___ Maturity Date: ___/___/___
Account Name: ______
Phone: (____)______
Website: ______
Picture or Pin: ______
Login information: UserName: ______
Password: ______

Name of Bank: ______
Phone: (____)______
Address: ______
______
Type of Bond/Account: ______
Value: $______ Serial #: ______
Issue Date: ___/___/___ Maturity Date: ___/___/___
Account Name: ______
Phone: (____)______
Website: ______
Picture or Pin: ______
Login information: UserName: ______
Password: ______

Name of Bank: ______
Phone: (____)______
Address: ______
______
Type of Bond/Account: ______
Value: $______ Serial #: ______
Issue Date: ___/___/___ Maturity Date: ___/___/___
Account Name: ______
Phone: (____)______
Website: ______
Picture or Pin: ______
Login information: UserName: ______
Password: ______

Name of Bank: ______
Phone: (____)______
Address: ______
______
Type of Bond/Account: ______
Value: $______ Serial #: ______
Issue Date: ___/___/___ Maturity Date: ___/___/___
Account Name: ______
Phone: (____)______
Website: ______
Picture or Pin: ______
Login information: UserName: ______
Password: ______

INFORMATION

(Please Don't Forget to CANCEL all Credit Cards in My Name!)

Credit Card Company: ______________________ Credit Card #: ________________
Type of card: [ ] Visa [ ] Mastercard [ ] Discover [ ] American Express [ ] Other: __________
Card holder Name: ______________________ Phone #: (________)______________
Address: ________________________ City, State, Zip: ______________________
Approximate Balance on Card: $____________
Website: ________________________________
Login information: UserName: ______________________Password: ______________

Credit Card Company: ______________________ Credit Card #: ________________
Type of card: [ ] Visa [ ] Mastercard [ ] Discover [ ] American Express [ ] Other: __________
Card holder Name: ______________________ Phone #: (________)______________
Address: ________________________ City, State, Zip: ______________________
Approximate Balance on Card: $____________
Website: ________________________________
Login information: UserName: ______________________Password: ______________

Credit Card Company: ______________________ Credit Card #: ________________
Type of card: [ ] Visa [ ] Mastercard [ ] Discover [ ] American Express [ ] Other: __________
Card holder Name: ______________________ Phone #: (________)______________
Address: ________________________ City, State, Zip: ______________________
Approximate Balance on Card: $____________
Website: ________________________________
Login information: UserName: ______________________Password: ______________

BILLS AND EXPENSES

Monthly Expenses

Company Name: ______________________
Phone: (_______)______________
Address: ______________________
____
Account #: ______________
Amount Due: $__________
Frequency of Payment(s): (M) ___ (Q) ___ (A) ___
Description of Bill/Expense: ______________
____
Website: ______________________
Login information: UserName: ______________
Password: ______________________

Company Name: ______________________
Phone: (_______)______________
Address: ______________________
____
Account #: ______________
Amount Due: $__________
Frequency of Payment(s): (M) ___ (Q) ___ (A) ___
Description of Bill/Expense: ______________
____
Website: ______________________
Login information: UserName: ______________
Password: ______________________

Company Name: ______________________
Phone: (_______)______________
Address: ______________________
____
Account #: ______________
Amount Due: $__________
Frequency of Payment(s): (M) ___ (Q) ___ (A) ___
Description of Bill/Expense: ______________
____
Website: ______________________
Login information: UserName: ______________
Password: ______________________

Company Name: ______________________
Phone: (_______)______________
Address: ______________________
____
Account #: ______________
Amount Due: $__________
Frequency of Payment(s): (M) ___ (Q) ___ (A) ___
Description of Bill/Expense: ______________
____
Website: ______________________
Login information: UserName: ______________
Password: ______________________

Company Name: ______________________
Phone: (_______)______________
Address: ______________________
____
Account #: ______________
Amount Due: $__________
Frequency of Payment(s): (M) ___ (Q) ___ (A) ___
Description of Bill/Expense: ______________
____
Website: ______________________
Login information: UserName: ______________
Password: ______________________

Company Name: ______________________
Phone: (_______)______________
Address: ______________________
____
Account #: ______________
Amount Due: $__________
Frequency of Payment(s): (M) ___ (Q) ___ (A) ___
Description of Bill/Expense: ______________
____
Website: ______________________
Login information: UserName: ______________
Password: ______________________

Monthly Expenses

Company Name: ____________________
Phone: (______)____________________
Address: ____________________

Account #: ____________________
Amount Due: $________________
Frequency of Payment(s): (M) ____ (Q) ____ (A) ____
Description of Bill/Expense: ____________________

Website: ____________________
Login information: UserName: ____________________
Password: ____________________

Company Name: ____________________
Phone: (______)____________________
Address: ____________________

Account #: ____________________
Amount Due: $________________
Frequency of Payment(s): (M) ____ (Q) ____ (A) ____
Description of Bill/Expense: ____________________

Website: ____________________
Login information: UserName: ____________________
Password: ____________________

Company Name: ____________________
Phone: (______)____________________
Address: ____________________

Account #: ____________________
Amount Due: $________________
Frequency of Payment(s): (M) ____ (Q) ____ (A) ____
Description of Bill/Expense: ____________________

Website: ____________________
Login information: UserName: ____________________
Password: ____________________

Company Name: ____________________
Phone: (______)____________________
Address: ____________________

Account #: ____________________
Amount Due: $________________
Frequency of Payment(s): (M) ____ (Q) ____ (A) ____
Description of Bill/Expense: ____________________

Website: ____________________
Login information: UserName: ____________________
Password: ____________________

Company Name: ____________________
Phone: (______)____________________
Address: ____________________

Account #: ____________________
Amount Due: $________________
Frequency of Payment(s): (M) ____ (Q) ____ (A) ____
Description of Bill/Expense: ____________________

Website: ____________________
Login information: UserName: ____________________
Password: ____________________

Company Name: ____________________
Phone: (______)____________________
Address: ____________________

Account #: ____________________
Amount Due: $________________
Frequency of Payment(s): (M) ____ (Q) ____ (A) ____
Description of Bill/Expense: ____________________

Website: ____________________
Login information: UserName: ____________________
Password: ____________________

Monthly Subscriptions

Company Name: ______________________
Phone: (______)____________________
Address: ______________________
____
Account #: ____________________
Amount Due: $__________
Frequency of Payment(s): (M) ___ (Q) ___ (A) ___
Description of Bill/Expense: ______________________
____
Website: ______________________
Login information: UserName: ______________________
Password: ______________________

Company Name: ______________________
Phone: (______)____________________
Address: ______________________
____
Account #: ____________________
Amount Due: $__________
Frequency of Payment(s): (M) ___ (Q) ___ (A) ___
Description of Bill/Expense: ______________________
____
Website: ______________________
Login information: UserName: ______________________
Password: ______________________

Company Name: ______________________
Phone: (______)____________________
Address: ______________________
____
Account #: ____________________
Amount Due: $__________
Frequency of Payment(s): (M) ___ (Q) ___ (A) ___
Description of Bill/Expense: ______________________
____
Website: ______________________
Login information: UserName: ______________________
Password: ______________________

Company Name: ______________________
Phone: (______)____________________
Address: ______________________
____
Account #: ____________________
Amount Due: $__________
Frequency of Payment(s): (M) ___ (Q) ___ (A) ___
Description of Bill/Expense: ______________________
____
Website: ______________________
Login information: UserName: ______________________
Password: ______________________

Company Name: ______________________
Phone: (______)____________________
Address: ______________________
____
Account #: ____________________
Amount Due: $__________
Frequency of Payment(s): (M) ___ (Q) ___ (A) ___
Description of Bill/Expense: ______________________
____
Website: ______________________
Login information: UserName: ______________________
Password: ______________________

Company Name: ______________________
Phone: (______)____________________
Address: ______________________
____
Account #: ____________________
Amount Due: $__________
Frequency of Payment(s): (M) ___ (Q) ___ (A) ___
Description of Bill/Expense: ______________________
____
Website: ______________________
Login information: UserName: ______________________
Password: ______________________

BUSINESSES

Business Contacts

LIST

Company: ______________________________
Name: ______________________________
Phone: (________)____________________
Address: ______________________________
____
Website: ______________________________
Email address: ______________________________
NOTES: ______________________________
____
____

Company: ______________________________
Name: ______________________________
Phone: (________)____________________
Address: ______________________________
____
Website: ______________________________
Email address: ______________________________
NOTES: ______________________________
____
____

Company: ______________________________
Name: ______________________________
Phone: (________)____________________
Address: ______________________________
____
Website: ______________________________
Email address: ______________________________
NOTES: ______________________________
____
____

Company: ______________________________
Name: ______________________________
Phone: (________)____________________
Address: ______________________________
____
Website: ______________________________
Email address: ______________________________
NOTES: ______________________________
____
____

Company: ______________________________
Name: ______________________________
Phone: (________)____________________
Address: ______________________________
____
Website: ______________________________
Email address: ______________________________
NOTES: ______________________________
____
____

Company: ______________________________
Name: ______________________________
Phone: (________)____________________
Address: ______________________________
____
Website: ______________________________
Email address: ______________________________
NOTES: ______________________________
____
____

Business Ownership
INFORMATION

Name of Business: ______________________________ EIN #: ______-______________
Address:____ Country: __________
Type of Business:______________________________ For Profit: ___ Not For Profit: ___
Owner(s) of Business: ______________________ Phone: (________)______________
Owner(s) of Business: ______________________ Phone: (________)______________
Owner(s) of Business: ______________________ Phone: (________)______________
License Required? Y ___N ___
Type of License (If applicable): __________________ License Number (If applicable): ______________
Website: ____________________ Email: ____________________________
Login information: UserName: __________________ Password: __________________________
NOTES: ____
____

Name of Business: ______________________________ EIN #: ______-______________
Address:____ Country: __________
Type of Business:______________________________ For Profit: ___ Not For Profit: ___
Owner(s) of Business: ______________________ Phone: (________)______________
Owner(s) of Business: ______________________ Phone: (________)______________
Owner(s) of Business: ______________________ Phone: (________)______________
License Required? Y ___N ___
Type of License (If applicable): __________________ License Number (If applicable): ______________
Website: ____________________ Email: ____________________________
Login information: UserName: __________________ Password: __________________________
NOTES: ____
____

Name of Business: ______________________________ EIN #: ______-______________
Address:____ Country: __________
Type of Business:______________________________ For Profit: ___ Not For Profit: ___
Owner(s) of Business: ______________________ Phone: (________)______________
Owner(s) of Business: ______________________ Phone: (________)______________
Owner(s) of Business: ______________________ Phone: (________)______________
License Required? Y ___N ___
Type of License (If applicable): __________________ License Number (If applicable): ______________
Website: ____________________ Email: ____________________________
Login information: UserName: __________________ Password: __________________________
NOTES: ____
____

Professional Contacts
LIST

Company: ______________________
Name: ______________________
Phone: (______)______________
Address: ______________________
____
Website: ______________________
Email address: ______________________
NOTES: ______________________
____
____

Company: ______________________
Name: ______________________
Phone: (______)______________
Address: ______________________
____
Website: ______________________
Email address: ______________________
NOTES: ______________________
____
____

Company: ______________________
Name: ______________________
Phone: (______)______________
Address: ______________________
____
Website: ______________________
Email address: ______________________
NOTES: ______________________
____
____

Company: ______________________
Name: ______________________
Phone: (______)______________
Address: ______________________
____
Website: ______________________
Email address: ______________________
NOTES: ______________________
____
____

Company: ______________________
Name: ______________________
Phone: (______)______________
Address: ______________________
____
Website: ______________________
Email address: ______________________
NOTES: ______________________
____
____

Company: ______________________
Name: ______________________
Phone: (______)______________
Address: ______________________
____
Website: ______________________
Email address: ______________________
NOTES: ______________________
____
____

REAL ESTATE

Real Estate Properties

INFORMATION

Property Address: ________________ County: ________________
Property Owner's Name: ________________ Phone: (________)________________
Type of Property: ___ Land ___ Single Family/Condo ___ Multi-Family ___ Commercial SqFt: ________
Value: $________________ Purchase Price: $________________ Mortgage?: ___ Y ___ N
Mortgage Holder: ________________ Phone: (________)________________
Account #: ________________ Monthly Payments: $________ Taxes: $________
Website: ________________ Email: ________________
Login information: UserName: ________________ Password: ________________

Property Address: ________________ County: ________________
Property Owner's Name: ________________ Phone: (________)________________
Type of Property: ___ Land ___ Single Family/Condo ___ Multi-Family ___ Commercial SqFt: ________
Value: $________________ Purchase Price: $________________ Mortgage?: ___ Y ___ N
Mortgage Holder: ________________ Phone: (________)________________
Account #: ________________ Monthly Payments: $________ Taxes: $________
Website: ________________ Email: ________________
Login information: UserName: ________________ Password: ________________

Property Address: ________________ County: ________________
Property Owner's Name: ________________ Phone: (________)________________
Type of Property: ___ Land ___ Single Family/Condo ___ Multi-Family ___ Commercial SqFt: ________
Value: $________________ Purchase Price: $________________ Mortgage?: ___ Y ___ N
Mortgage Holder: ________________ Phone: (________)________________
Account #: ________________ Monthly Payments: $________ Taxes: $________
Website: ________________ Email: ________________
Login information: UserName: ________________ Password: ________________

Property Address: ________________ County: ________________
Property Owner's Name: ________________ Phone: (________)________________
Type of Property: ___ Land ___ Single Family/Condo ___ Multi-Family ___ Commercial SqFt: ________
Value: $________________ Purchase Price: $________________ Mortgage?: ___ Y ___ N
Mortgage Holder: ________________ Phone: (________)________________
Account #: ________________ Monthly Payments: $________ Taxes: $________
Website: ________________ Email: ________________
Login information: UserName: ________________ Password: ________________

Real Estate Properties

INFORMATION

Property Address: ______________________ County: ______________
Property Owner's Name: ______________________ Phone: (________)______________
Type of Property: ___ Land ___ Single Family/Condo ___ Multi-Family ___ Commercial SqFt: __________
Value: $______________ Purchase Price: $______________ Mortgage?: ___ Y ___ N
Mortgage Holder: ______________________ Phone: (________)______________
Account #: ______________ Monthly Payments: $__________ Taxes: $__________
Website: ______________________ Email: ______________________
Login information: UserName: ______________ Password: ______________

Property Address: ______________________ County: ______________
Property Owner's Name: ______________________ Phone: (________)______________
Type of Property: ___ Land ___ Single Family/Condo ___ Multi-Family ___ Commercial SqFt: __________
Value: $______________ Purchase Price: $______________ Mortgage?: ___ Y ___ N
Mortgage Holder: ______________________ Phone: (________)______________
Account #: ______________ Monthly Payments: $__________ Taxes: $__________
Website: ______________________ Email: ______________________
Login information: UserName: ______________ Password: ______________

Property Address: ______________________ County: ______________
Property Owner's Name: ______________________ Phone: (________)______________
Type of Property: ___ Land ___ Single Family/Condo ___ Multi-Family ___ Commercial SqFt: __________
Value: $______________ Purchase Price: $______________ Mortgage?: ___ Y ___ N
Mortgage Holder: ______________________ Phone: (________)______________
Account #: ______________ Monthly Payments: $__________ Taxes: $__________
Website: ______________________ Email: ______________________
Login information: UserName: ______________ Password: ______________

Property Address: ______________________ County: ______________
Property Owner's Name: ______________________ Phone: (________)______________
Type of Property: ___ Land ___ Single Family/Condo ___ Multi-Family ___ Commercial SqFt: __________
Value: $______________ Purchase Price: $______________ Mortgage?: ___ Y ___ N
Mortgage Holder: ______________________ Phone: (________)______________
Account #: ______________ Monthly Payments: $__________ Taxes: $__________
Website: ______________________ Email: ______________________
Login information: UserName: ______________ Password: ______________

Real Estate Rentals
INFORMATION

Tenant information: ______________________ Phone: (________)______________
Property Address: ______________________ County: ______________
Property Owner's Name: ______________________ Phone: (________)______________
Type of Property: ___ Land ___ Single Family/Condo ___ Multi-Family ___ Commercial SqFt: __________
Monthly Rental: $__________ Long Term or Short Term?: __________ Lease?: ___Y ___ N
Mortgage Holder: ______________________ Phone: (________)______________
Account #: ______________ Monthly Payments: $________ Taxes: $________
Website: ______________________ Email: ______________________
Login information: UserName: ______________ Password: ______________________

Tenant information: ______________________ Phone: (________)______________
Property Address: ______________________ County: ______________
Property Owner's Name: ______________________ Phone: (________)______________
Type of Property: ___ Land ___ Single Family/Condo ___ Multi-Family ___ Commercial SqFt: __________
Monthly Rental: $__________ Long Term or Short Term?: __________ Lease?: ___Y ___ N
Mortgage Holder: ______________________ Phone: (________)______________
Account #: ______________ Monthly Payments: $________ Taxes: $________
Website: ______________________ Email: ______________________
Login information: UserName: ______________ Password: ______________________

Tenant information: ______________________ Phone: (________)______________
Property Address: ______________________ County: ______________
Property Owner's Name: ______________________ Phone: (________)______________
Type of Property: ___ Land ___ Single Family/Condo ___ Multi-Family ___ Commercial SqFt: __________
Monthly Rental: $__________ Long Term or Short Term?: __________ Lease?: ___Y ___ N
Mortgage Holder: ______________________ Phone: (________)______________
Account #: ______________ Monthly Payments: $________ Taxes: $________
Website: ______________________ Email: ______________________
Login information: UserName: ______________ Password: ______________________

INFORMATION

Tenant information: ______________________________ Phone: (________)______________
Property Address: ______________________________ County: ______________
Property Owner's Name: ______________________________ Phone: (________)______________
Type of Property: ___ Land ___ Single Family/Condo ___ Multi-Family ___ Commercial SqFt: __________
Monthly Rental: $______________ Long Term or Short Term?: ______________ Lease?: ___Y ___ N
Mortgage Holder: ______________________________ Phone: (________)______________
Account #: ______________ Monthly Payments: $__________ Taxes: $__________
Website: ______________________________ Email: ______________________________
Login information: UserName: ______________________ Password: ______________________

Tenant information: ______________________________ Phone: (________)______________
Property Address: ______________________________ County: ______________
Property Owner's Name: ______________________________ Phone: (________)______________
Type of Property: ___ Land ___ Single Family/Condo ___ Multi-Family ___ Commercial SqFt: __________
Monthly Rental: $______________ Long Term or Short Term?: ______________ Lease?: ___Y ___ N
Mortgage Holder: ______________________________ Phone: (________)______________
Account #: ______________ Monthly Payments: $__________ Taxes: $__________
Website: ______________________________ Email: ______________________________
Login information: UserName: ______________________ Password: ______________________

Tenant information: ______________________________ Phone: (________)______________
Property Address: ______________________________ County: ______________
Property Owner's Name: ______________________________ Phone: (________)______________
Type of Property: ___ Land ___ Single Family/Condo ___ Multi-Family ___ Commercial SqFt: __________
Monthly Rental: $______________ Long Term or Short Term?: ______________ Lease?: ___Y ___ N
Mortgage Holder: ______________________________ Phone: (________)______________
Account #: ______________ Monthly Payments: $__________ Taxes: $__________
Website: ______________________________ Email: ______________________________
Login information: UserName: ______________________ Password: ______________________

INSURANCES

INFORMATION

Life Insurance Company: ______________________ Policy Number: ________________

Name of Insured: ______________________ Date of Birth: ____/____/____ Sex: ___ M ___ F

Owner of Policy: ______________________ Phone: (____)________________

Type of Policy: ___ Term Life ___ Whole Life ___ Universal Life Other: ______________

Amount of Policy: $__________ Payments: $__________ (M) ___ (Q) ___ (A) ___

Website: ______________________

Login information: UserName: ______________________ Password: ________________

Beneficiaries: Primary (P) or Contingent (C)

Name: ______________________ Percentage: ________ % (____)

Name: ______________________ Percentage: ________ % (____)

Name: ______________________ Percentage: ________ % (____)

Name: ______________________ Percentage: ________ % (____)

Life Insurance Company: ______________________ Policy Number: ________________

Name of Insured: ______________________ Date of Birth: ____/____/____ Sex: ___ M ___ F

Owner of Policy: ______________________ Phone: (____)________________

Type of Policy: ___ Term Life ___ Whole Life ___ Universal Life Other: ______________

Amount of Policy: $__________ Payments: $__________ (M) ___ (Q) ___ (A) ___

Website: ______________________

Login information: UserName: ______________________ Password: ________________

Beneficiaries: Primary (P) or Contingent (C)

Name: ______________________ Percentage: ________ % (____)

Name: ______________________ Percentage: ________ % (____)

Name: ______________________ Percentage: ________ % (____)

Name: ______________________ Percentage: ________ % (____)

Life Insurance Company: ______________________ Policy Number: ________________

Name of Insured: ______________________ Date of Birth: ____/____/____ Sex: ___ M ___ F

Owner of Policy: ______________________ Phone: (____)________________

Type of Policy: ___ Term Life ___ Whole Life ___ Universal Life Other: ______________

Amount of Policy: $__________ Payments: $__________ (M) ___ (Q) ___ (A) ___

Website: ______________________

Login information: UserName: ______________________ Password: ________________

Beneficiaries: Primary (P) or Contingent (C)

Name: ______________________ Percentage: ________ % (____)

Name: ______________________ Percentage: ________ % (____)

Name: ______________________ Percentage: ________ % (____)

Name: ______________________ Percentage: ________ % (____)

Real Estate Insurance

INFORMATION

Insured property address: ______ County: ______
Property Record: ______ Insurance Company: ______
Phone: (____)______
Coverage info: ______ Policy number: ______
Deductible: ______ Premium: $______
Agent info: ______ Phone: (____)______
Agent email: ______
NOTES: ______

Insured property address: ______ County: ______
Property Record: ______ Insurance Company: ______
Phone: (____)______
Coverage info: ______ Policy number: ______
Deductible: ______ Premium: $______
Agent info: ______ Phone: (____)______
Agent email: ______
NOTES: ______

Insured property address: ______ County: ______
Property Record: ______ Insurance Company: ______
Phone: (____)______
Coverage info: ______ Policy number: ______
Deductible: ______ Premium: $______
Agent info: ______ Phone: (____)______
Agent email: ______
NOTES: ______

Real Estate Insurance

INFORMATION

Insured property address: ______________________ County: ______________
Property Record: ______________ Insurance Company: ______________________
Phone: (______)______________
Coverage info: ______________ Policy number: ______________
Deductible: ______________ Premium: $______________
Agent info: ______________ Phone: (______)______________
Agent email: ______________
NOTES: ____
____

Insured property address: ______________________ County: ______________
Property Record: ______________ Insurance Company: ______________________
Phone: (______)______________
Coverage info: ______________ Policy number: ______________
Deductible: ______________ Premium: $______________
Agent info: ______________ Phone: (______)______________
Agent email: ______________
NOTES: ____
____

Insured property address: ______________________ County: ______________
Property Record: ______________ Insurance Company: ______________________
Phone: (______)______________
Coverage info: ______________ Policy number: ______________
Deductible: ______________ Premium: $______________
Agent info: ______________ Phone: (______)______________
Agent email: ______________
NOTES: ____
____

ASSETS

INFORMATION

Owner's Name: ______________________ Phone: (______)______________
Address: ____
Make/Model of Car: ______________________ Color: ____________
Vehicle Tag: ______________ VIN #: ______________________
Payment Status: ___ Paid Off ___ Y ___ N
Financed with: ______________________ Monthly Amount: $____________
Insurance Company: ______________________ Phone: (______)______________

Owner's Name: ______________________ Phone: (______)______________
Address: ____
Make/Model of Car: ______________________ Color: ____________
Vehicle Tag: ______________ VIN #: ______________________
Payment Status: ___ Paid Off ___ Y ___ N
Financed with: ______________________ Monthly Amount: $____________
Insurance Company: ______________________ Phone: (______)______________

Owner's Name: ______________________ Phone: (______)______________
Address: ____
Make/Model of Car: ______________________ Color: ____________
Vehicle Tag: ______________ VIN #: ______________________
Payment Status: ___ Paid Off ___ Y ___ N
Financed with: ______________________ Monthly Amount: $____________
Insurance Company: ______________________ Phone: (______)______________

Owner's Name: ______________________ Phone: (______)______________
Address: ____
Make/Model of Car: ______________________ Color: ____________
Vehicle Tag: ______________ VIN #: ______________________
Payment Status: ___ Paid Off ___ Y ___ N
Financed with: ______________________ Monthly Amount: $____________
Insurance Company: ______________________ Phone: (______)______________

Stocks & Commodities
INFORMATION

Brokerage Information	Name of Stock	Ticker Symbol	Quantity	Market Value

Crypto and Digital Assets

Platform: ______________________________
Website: ______________________________
PIN #: ____________
Login information:
UserName: ______________________
Password: ________________

Platform: ______________________________
Website: ______________________________
PIN #: ____________
Login information:
UserName: ______________________
Password: ________________

Platform: ______________________________
Website: ______________________________
PIN #: ____________
Login information:
UserName: ______________________
Password: ________________

Platform: ______________________________
Website: ______________________________
PIN #: ____________
Login information:
UserName: ______________________
Password: ________________

Hardware Wallet information:
Password: ______________________________
Type: ______________________________
PIN #: ____________ 2FA PIN #: ____________

SEED WORDS:

1	2	3	4	5	6
7	8	9	10	11	12
13	14	15	16	17	18
19	20	21	22	23	24

Hardware Wallet information:
Password: ______________________________
Type: ______________________________
PIN #: ____________ 2FA PIN #: ____________

SEED WORDS:

1	2	3	4	5	6
7	8	9	10	11	12
13	14	15	16	17	18
19	20	21	22	23	24

Types of Crypto Currency

Platform	Name of Crypto	Ticker Info	Quantity	Market Value	Location of Asset
				$	
				$	
				$	
				$	
				$	
				$	
				$	
				$	
				$	
				$	
				$	
				$	
				$	
				$	
				$	
				$	
				$	
				$	
				$	

Furniture and Belongings

Name of Item	Description	Color	Unit	Market Value	Location of Asset
				$	
				$	
				$	
				$	
				$	
				$	
				$	
				$	
				$	
				$	
				$	
				$	
				$	
				$	
				$	
				$	
				$	
				$	
				$	

Art & Precious Jewelry

Name of Item	Description	Size	Quantity	Market Value	Location of Asset
				$	
				$	
				$	
				$	
				$	
				$	
				$	
				$	
				$	
				$	
				$	
				$	
				$	
				$	
				$	
				$	
				$	
				$	
				$	

PET CARE

INFORMATION

GENERAL INFORMATION

Pet Name: ______________________________

Date of Birth: ______________________________

Place of Birth: ______________________________

Sex: ____ M ____ F

Breed: ______________________________

Color/Markings: ______________________________

License/Tag #: ______________________________

Microchip #: ______________________________

VET INFORMATION

Name: ______________________________ Phone (________)______________________

Email: ______________________________

Address: ______________________________

FEEDING AND CARE

Food Brand/Type: ______________________________

Eating schedule: ______________________________

Potty schedule: ______________________________

Sleeping schedule: ______________________________

Likes or dislikes: ______________________________

Favorite toy(s): ______________________________

Triggers: ______________________________

WHO GETS THE PET?

Name: ______________________________ Phone (________)______________________

Email: ______________________________

INFORMATION

GENERAL INFORMATION

Pet Name: ______________________________
Date of Birth: ____________________________
Place of Birth: ___________________________
Sex: ____ M ____ F

Breed: __________________________________
Color/Markings: __________________________
License/Tag #: ___________________________
Microchip #: _____________________________

VET INFORMATION

Name: ____________________________________ Phone (_______)______________________
Email: ____
Address: ____

FEEDING AND CARE

Food Brand/Type: ____
Eating schedule: ____
Potty schedule: ____
Sleeping schedule: ____
Likes or dislikes: ____
Favorite toy(s): ____
Triggers: ____

WHO GETS THE PET?

Name: ____________________________________ Phone (_______)______________________
Email: ____

DOMAINS & WEBSITES

DOMAIN NAMES	DOMAIN NAMES	DOMAIN NAMES

Field	Entry
Hosting:	
Website:	
Username:	
Password:	

Field	Entry
Hosting:	
Website:	
Username:	
Password:	

Field	Entry
Hosting:	
Website:	
Username:	
Password:	

Field	Entry
Hosting:	
Website:	
Username:	
Password:	

Field	Entry
Hosting:	
Website:	
Username:	
Password:	

Field	Entry
Hosting:	
Website:	
Username:	
Password:	

Field	Entry
Hosting:	
Website:	
Username:	
Password:	

Field	Entry
Hosting:	
Website:	
Username:	
Password:	

Field	Entry
Hosting:	
Website:	
Username:	
Password:	

Field	Entry
Hosting:	
Website:	
Username:	
Password:	

Field	Entry
Hosting:	
Website:	
Username:	
Password:	

Field	Entry
Hosting:	
Website:	
Username:	
Password:	

PASSWORDS

Password Tracker

Website: ______________________________
Username: ____________________________
Password: _____________________________

Website: ______________________________
Username: ____________________________
Password: _____________________________

Website: ______________________________
Username: ____________________________
Password: _____________________________

Website: ______________________________
Username: ____________________________
Password: _____________________________

Website: ______________________________
Username: ____________________________
Password: _____________________________

Website: ______________________________
Username: ____________________________
Password: _____________________________

Website: ______________________________
Username: ____________________________
Password: _____________________________

Website: ______________________________
Username: ____________________________
Password: _____________________________

Website: ______________________________
Username: ____________________________
Password: _____________________________

Website: ______________________________
Username: ____________________________
Password: _____________________________

Password Tracker

Website: ______________________
Username: ______________________
Password: ______________________

Website: ______________________
Username: ______________________
Password: ______________________

Website: ______________________
Username: ______________________
Password: ______________________

Website: ______________________
Username: ______________________
Password: ______________________

Website: ______________________
Username: ______________________
Password: ______________________

Website: ______________________
Username: ______________________
Password: ______________________

Website: ______________________
Username: ______________________
Password: ______________________

Website: ______________________
Username: ______________________
Password: ______________________

Website: ______________________
Username: ______________________
Password: ______________________

Website: ______________________
Username: ______________________
Password: ______________________

NOTES

Notes

Estate Planning Publishers

DATE :

Notes

Estate Planning Publishers

DATE :

Get Your Affairs in Order Today—Because Tomorrow Is Never Promised.

Don't leave your family guessing. Too many people pass away unexpectedly, leaving loved ones with no knowledge of their assets, wishes, or important documents.

A Family Estate Planning Record Book gives your family clarity, prevents legal headaches, and brings peace of mind—both for you and those you care about most.

What is Estate Planning?
Estate planning is the process of clearly organizing your property, assets, and personal wishes so they can be smoothly transferred to your loved ones after your passing.

It is best approached proactively—before illness or life's unexpected turns make it more difficult to update or manage. The earlier you start, the more control and confidence you'll have.

Your plan should be reviewed annually, and especially during times of major life change or illness.

Why This Record Book Matters:
■ Saves your family from legal disputes
■ Provides clear guidance when emotions run high
■ Keeps your legacy intact
■ Gives your loved ones peace of mind in uncertain times
Don't wait until it's too late. Give your family the gift of preparation, clarity, and security with this comprehensive Estate Planning Record Book.

Congratulations—by taking this step, you're protecting your loved ones and ensuring your legacy.

☛ Visit: www.estateplanningpublishers.com

Made in the USA
Columbia, SC
25 July 2025